CONTENTS

Spirit Poems
"Above Every Mountain There is Light"

Written by
Steven Schluepner

Dedication

I dedicate this book to my
Spiritual and Life Coach, Steve D'Annunzio,
my High School Track and Field Coach Greg Krupa,
my caring and thoughtful friend
Dale Diver, who is no longer with us,
and all of the people who played
shaping roles in my life. I would also like to
honor those who tested, hurt,
abandoned, and manipulated me.
Without all of you, and your critical influence,
the poems would have little purpose.

~God Bless, Steve

The Poems

*"To work with silence is to work
with the language of God."*

*~Carolyn Myss
Author, "Entering the Castle"*

These poems came from my time in silence. It's that self-reflection, and intentional work around inviting the complex emotions rising from the pain and loss around my divorce to teach me, that spawned the poems.   The poems are gifts of understanding. They gave me answers that :

opened my eyes to why the suffering is here,

helped me understand the divine guidance within the upset, and

showed me new pathways to personal growth and knowing myself.

I share them with you because I believe they have the ability to speak across a wide range of life challenges.

Understanding Loss

Loss

Laugh at Loss.
It's impossible to lose,
what we don't have

houses
careers
others
money
are not ours

They can be gone in an instant
through events beyond our control.
Therefore, we never had them,
only existed with them.

What you have can never be lost

heart
wisdom
knowledge
love
peace

These are yours for life.
Yet, we trade them for things
we could never have.
In that trade,
we unconsciously loan them away.

Cherish Thorns

Being used and exploited
Being used to fill missing needs
Having power and identity stolen
Having emasculation steal confidence
Losing family and friends
Losing what once was – good or bad
Is all damaging
Is all scar producing

It's okay to reflect on these thorns
It's okay to allow them to wrap your garden
For if not the thorns
the garden would not exist
would not grow and produce fruit safely

The deeper the hurt
the richer the soil
The deeper the lessons
the more fantastic the garden
I wish to blend my garden with yours
I cherish the thorns.

Rock Bottom

What does it mean to hit Rock Bottom?
It's when we reach the end
of a belief system.
A belief system that imprisons
one from being oneself.
Lessons in life repeat with greater
severity until learned.
My Rock Bottom came with the loss
of my family.
Divorce forced me to relinquish
a futile belief system.
One centered on driving for success
and achievement and proving.
Cover-ups of low self-esteem and
lack of love for me.
Rock Bottom, as painful as it was,
was a miracle.
For when I lifted the Rock
I found a profound truth
I found me.

Cultivate Miracles

Sit in awe of your miracles.
Miracles that change one to the core.
Core growth that sprouts more.
More miracles which shape our being.
Being alive merely means we will be stripped.
Stripped of the perceived needs of life.
Life has a way of removing when learning is needed.
Needed lessons are necessary for miracles to rise.
Rise from the spirit and truth.
Truth is the miracle for it cannot be bad.
Bad happens when truth is hidden.
Hidden miracles flourish when truth is cultivated.

Stained Glass

In a blink of an eye
she was gone.
Remnants of a life shared
seeded and scattered
for the eye to see.
With each item attached a memory
unique to me.
Some gifts, some milestones.
Memories deriving meaning.

As I look at the stained glass,
blues and greens casting a memory
out the window of time,
thoughts of Christmas – her gift
left for me to bear.

Its meaning left with each passing day.
Today it is beautiful art, made with love
lighting a room with blues and green.

Ruler of Want

lack is the rough, dingy, hard
edge around want
as long as want is wrapped with lack
she will hide in the cusp of opportunity
lack is living in the valley on the journey to want
the lacking journey does not end
because thoughts of lack confuse the universe
to believe they are thoughts of want

true want is a disbelief in lack
a soft, bright possibility around want
showing herself in the face of opportunity
the ruler sits at the peak of want
with eyes lifted over every valley

Sitting With Sadness

Weeping

Weeping.
Hands raised to receive
On knees holding the weight of me
Tears flow as spirit bereaves
My strength is in my weakness.

Weeping.
Lessons carved in my soul
Certain all pain is good
For all to reveal the important tolls
My strength is in my weakness.

Weeping.
Seeing new faces appear
People to guide me
With gentle nudges towards fear
My strength is in my weakness.

Weeping.
Children blossoming into their own
Stretching their boundaries
Confidence is known
My strength is in my weakness.

Weeping.
For the feeling of love
Bouncing from heart to heart
As gentle as a dove
My strength is in my weakness.

Hurt Anchor

My chakras are in flux,
giving warning signs for healing.
I can tell by the tightness in my chest and throat
and the toiling in my stomach.
Please guide me. Show me
how to heal this.

Remember, the cause of the upset
is never what we are experiencing now.
The cause drifts back
to a much earlier wound.
Possibly from a childhood hurt
around being dropped or replaced or chastised.
The sign causing the angst and hurt
is your soul asking for healing
from your judgement of yourself,
from your willing view to see
yourself lacking or inferior.
Don't suppress the discomfort, as it
will just resurface later, and
with greater effect.
Sit with the emotion, and ask
to be shown the cause.
Only then will you be able to release
your hurt anchor and heal.

Sealing Chambers of Pain

The pulsating energy envelops me
from my crown
to my grounded oneness.
Going deep into forgiveness
creates voids.
Voids housed by pain.
It's not possible to let voids exist
for if one does, they will re-fill
with painful memories.
As the Archangels give this great
healing gift –
the gift you will be keenly aware
from the energy passing through you –
Fill the void.
Fill it with love for you.
Love the images of the little boy
as he turns to the man he is.
This awareness, this love,
seals those chambers of pain.

Knot of Pain

Look not through
the knot hole of your pain,
look at the knot.

Peace Instant

The space between an inhale and exhale,
The closed and open side of a blink,
Between each heartbeat,
Is the chase for peace.
It's the instant, now.
It's not the retirement account, or college fund,
The fear of losing a loved one,
Or any storm on the horizon.
It's not the Facebook memory,
Or thought of a past pleasure or pain,
Nor the dream of some future better than today.
It's the gratitude for what is here, now
And the recognition you have what you are supposed to
at this time.
As soon as the energy attaches to any of these,
As soon as the story of illusion unfolds
and runs through the chambers of our mind,
the Peace Instant is gone.

Patience

Patience arrives so gently
She calms our hearts
Trying to tell us "All is Well"
Breathe and enjoy your moment
A Holy Instant, smiles and contentment
Inhale Life, and exhale fear
Patience is a gentle gift

Bodies resist patience, fight her quest
He twists our hearts, pushes to go
Trying to tell us "Acquire and compete"
Short breaths, fuel the angst
The Instant becomes fear
From the sense of lack for what is not
If only he knew patience is a gentle gift.

Beyond Meaning

Meaning brings certainty
Certainty we seek
Seek the path of God
God is not in meaning
Meaning is an attached story
Stories surround all we see
See the block to God
God is with us now, not in the past

Timeless Day

we spend this day together
You and I, alone
with a soft peaceful breath
and a fearless mind
our work is paying fruit
that nurtures and strengthens
weakness disappears
as does time
today's experience is timeless

A Rich Journey

Journeys can traverse seas of sorrow.
They can carve stone so strong,
they meld one's mind into illusion.
They can stall in headwinds of fear,
and take on waves of tears.

With faith, and a divine hand,
a Journey can catch trade winds,
and whirl across glass waters,
so swiftly,
that soulmates are bonded,
and hearts see around granite peaks,
into a horizon holding nothing,
but the vast light of love.

A Journey like this
is a rich Journey, indeed!

Facing Obligation

A Reflection Back

as you look in the mirror
see beyond the image
peer into the soul
feel your breath
but don't let it fog the glass
every wrinkle around the eye
is evidence of a life lived
recognize the grace
for who you are today
see the beauty of your being
as your beauty was shaped
through the unity of all
past relationships and experiences
each event caused your beauty
your job is to accept the beauty you see
remember, the mirror of life
is a reflection back

Peace Stealers

Peace stealers.
Mind thieves that rob joy
from our lives.
Daily we wake and are forced
to protect ourselves from
peace stealers.
Robbers in the form of colleagues,
neighbors, family members.
Thiefs over airwaves, in our
political system,
and through wanting more as others
post on social media.
Peace is stolen when we drift
from God's love.
Recognize the triggers
that steal peace.
Then remember that no one,
no one,
can steal peace,
if we don't allow ourselves
to drift.

Dream Lifters

There are invisible boxes
that capture dreams.
They float as views
expressed by another –
most likely a loved one.
The words attract the dream
in a magnetic way.

Some dreams never go further,
for the words have netted
the dream, and stored it
in the box of never-hood.
The box is sealed, and the dreamer
moves on to endure
the nightmare of regret.

Some dreamers are so wise,
they keep their dreams within,
so dream stealers search other places.
They only share their dreams
with dream-lifters, who transport
the dream to new heights,
and prepare the dream for life.

Shameless Cynics

who are we, shameless cynics
capturing darkness in what we watch and read,
sentimental to forgiveness, as a
sign of weakness,
pointing to impure motives, hidden schemes
distrust of potential joy, love
cynics find these views, and
highlight their own low self-esteem,
fearful of complete vulnerability
to receive light in the darkest corners
to receive forgiveness, and repentance
to allow true community, in the
arms of the beloved
cynics build walls for a fight that
has yet to exist, or may never
what a day it would be if your
forgiveness is mine,
repentance is mine,
gifts are mine,
without comparison or jealousy
but with complete unity

Cat

When the cat chases the gazelle,
does he pick the less educated one?
Is it the one with the different coat?
Or, the one that seems to be content by himself?
Despite all that may exist,
the cat chooses weakness,
as nature's instinct to self-serve.
How did the gazelle form its strength?
Was it born with it?
Was it coupled with others as they run as a herd?
Maybe it's from the pursuits of the past
where its limits were tested and crossed?
The Cat of Life preys on weakness
and when its belly lies empty,
she will raise her head and feed once again.

Preventing Hurt

Rex

Rex was my friend
my link to peace and joy
excited to see me always
as I him.
He was my confidant in alone times
and my friend among friends.
When my parents divorced
his world changed.
He gladly uprooted his home
and accepted his new space.
He became my counsellor
my grieving partner.
I was crushed when he was gone
uprooted and given away
without even a good-bye.
My grief had nowhere to go
it went low – suppressed.
As change kept coming
adapting to new stopping points
my grief dissipated.
I thought.
What also dissipated
was my ability to grieve.
I had to learn how to swallow feelings
as I have to this day
four decades later.
Child trauma will cascade
and always be with you
until released and forgiven.

Bear

happily scratching his back on the sand
the cub rolls in contentment
and love for himself
loved ones who once caused hurt
look with amazed eyes, wanting
to touch the cub
a monster roar comes
from down the shoreline
the boundary bear rises and
sprints toward those reaching
not wanting to have anyone hurt
the little boy within again

Strong

Strong.
Granite seams of consciousness
Conviction to do right
Voices of confidence
Guiding days to night.

Strong.
Flexible like the Yew
Not wavering in shadows
Voices of confidence
Reaching Heaven's meadows.

Strong.
Foundations for family
Rooting deep in Sons' souls
Voices of confidence
Understanding a Father's role.

Strong.
A rose stemming an open flower
Love at its start
Voices of confidence
Holding tender hearts.

Father's Gift

As my son sits on my lap
leaning his back on my chest
and my arms wrapped
in Fatherly love,
I feel his heart beat
a soft patter.
A tear comes to my eye
as I think of his future
and the impression
I'm making on him.
My throat tightens.
I wonder if I'm doing right,
as I think about decisions,
my actions that roll to his view.
I want to hold on and protect
very well knowing
that will just harm.
Suddenly he turns
with a slightly crooked smile
and a glimmer of love
in his eye.
Without any words, he says
all is okay.

Provider Anxiety,
Father Nurturer

With your pale dangling from your
thick fingers, and sweat
permeating the dirt on your shirt,
I see honor on your exhausted face,
for the end of another day's
work.

Sacrifice, endurance, commitment
are the cornerstones of your life.

So proud of my hero, yet so distant.
Why couldn't you ease up?
Was it provider anxiety?
It must have been all you knew!

Fathers clasp onto these illusions
when their sons are born.
They too must work and provide.
Sacrifice for the pride!

Adopting their Father's image, or
tone, or essence, becomes
part of paternal identity.

Some break free, and carve a
different road,
causing confusion from a Father
who doesn't understand.

Nurture your heart, Fathers.
Recognize providing is not the
only love, sacrifice

is not the only love, endurance
is not the only love.

Nurture your paternal heart
with kindness, vulnerability,
acceptance, ease, and
tears, as you remember not
only the visible teachings
of your Father, but the
the inherent teaching of what not to do.

Meet your pride where they are,
and lift them up.
Help them explore new interests
while keeping them save and
healthy.
Allow them to come into their own
Under your nurturing heart.
Be a Father, and sometimes
a Mother.

A Deep Love for You Child

I cannot live my life
loving you more than me
my circumstances had me
carrying another's pain
I cannot live my life
loving you, carrying this pain, over me
the hurt anchor had to be cut
so I can love me
with the anchor goes the cord to you
it has to, so I can love me
Child, I have to love me more than you
so I can give you my best love
a deeper love than the love
tied to the anchor

The Oak Trees

The tall oak looks at its sapling
Straighten your trunk, so your roots
can grow.

But you're blocking my light
with your huge canopy.
I have to bend so I can see.

If you don't straighten your trunk
your whole life will be crooked.
You can't sustain strong winds
and the earth's pull
if your base is bowed.

If I don't see the light now
I will have to wait until your gone.
By then I will be dropping acorns of my own,
and they might be too weak to grow.

I've lived for one-hundred years, I know
the importance of a strong base.
I've seen much that you haven't.

The past is gone, my strong
provider of life.
Those storms will not be the same.
My roots will support my crooked base.

What I need now is the light.
I need to taste it now.

It will guide my growth as
it is meant to.
It will prepare me
for future storms and all
causes that could
have me fall.

My and I

my career, my money, my knowledge,
my way,
my, my, my
My's and I's separate
as cells separate to form cancer
My's and I's are often used with
I have to's, and I need to's
obligatory words to indicate
we are driving the ship
does the sun just shine on you?
do drops of rain only bear your name?
these touch us all, and come from
a creation beyond your control
shine your love and rain your wisdom
to benefit all, because they too
come from beyond your control
and as they do
feel your pulse of joy as your blood
becomes one with your brother

Uncertainty & Unfairness

Relax the Wanting Mind

Breath becomes short as my heart restricts
furrowed brows focus the mind
as molars clinch and grind,
on the endless want that binds.

Will this deliver the want?
Maybe so,
But, if so, will the path of truth be here?

Wisdom says not to fight currents.
Let the water take you to the new shore.
Patiently glide over rapids with
head held high.
Let faith and vision pore.
Relax the wanting mind,
For only God's hand will breathe
life on the truthful shores.

Vulnerability

Vulnerable is deemed to be
a bad state
a state of openness to
attack, deception, and loss.
A situation resulting in win-lose.

Rather it is joined with courage
to not fight or flight fear.
Courage to face fear is needed
to conquer illusions of mind.

Reach for vulnerability.
Embrace its truth
and do so only with awareness
for without scars appear.

Shining Feathers

The feathers of a peacock
shine in their uniqueness.
They fan and show brilliance,
magnificence like no other.
Peacocks digest thorns
so their feathers can cast wonder.
This makes me think
of the thorns I have eaten.
Are my feathers shining, or
are the thorns sticking to my soul?

Prodigal Son

The Prodigal Son returns home
in his father's beloved grace
A wastrel, lacking faith and
seizing control of idolatry

The Prodigal Son kneels in release
in his father's beloved embrace
A prodigy of love, full of faith,
and detachment from control

The Father holding sons with love
through his own father's beloved embrace
A teacher, of inner peace
To those seeking their own prodigal journey

We May Never Realize

We may never realize
what is right or wrong
for our attitude and responses
shape these answers.
We know not sweet without sour
beauty without ugly
purity without tarnish
strength without weak moments
learning without lessons
joy without discomfort
love without broken hearts.
We may never realize
what is what, without the other.

Discomfort Strong

life's imbalance breeds discomfort
oh, what a grating feeling
an uneasiness deep in my gut
instinct inclines to push it away
to rid it in any which way
quick and haste decisions are easy, but wrong
patience is needed as discomfort strong

concern, general or specific
with the former the worse
toiling in scenarios
uncontrollables curse
faith is needed as discomfort strong

fear, doubt, and worry
paralyzing thoughts on oneself
dreams become blurry
as potential sits on the shelf
confidence is needed as discomfort strong

achievement, pride, and excess
markings of true success
unappreciative feeling within
selfishness and materialism
drifting towards core sin
awareness is needed as discomfort strong

patience
faith
confidence
awareness
being fully present when comfort strong

...If I Break

nock plied on a string, a cord
tied to an arch of Yew wood, resilient
pull me Dear Lord, bend me
so my arrow will sail, through light
I don't care if I break
the dastard is fighting, clawing
my soul, little does he know
I don't care if I break

Rest in My Fatherly Embrace

My accounts are a pittance of what once was.
I rest in my fatherly embrace.
My children absorb a new world
I find hard to understand.
I rest in my fatherly embrace.
Possessions decay and falter, from where
do I get currency to replace.
I rest in my fatherly embrace.
Brothers attacking brothers at every corner
self-serving and acting on fears.
I rest in my fatherly embrace.
Memories of childhood trauma and past
pains change the negative thought.
I rest in my fatherly embrace.
Love that once was, exiting the vows
and the inherent dreams.
I rest in my fatherly embrace.
Resting in my fatherly embrace,
I can laugh at these storms
seeing that they have no effect
at loosening our embrace.

Emptiness & Loss

Scream a Purpose

Screams inside
Screams from my Soul
At my Soul
AHHHHHH!
Thoughts of missteps
And confused stagnation
Lost opportunities and
Lost relationships
Loss of peace and purpose
AHHHHHH!

Release the Screams
For the past is gone
Only memories of lessons remain
Stop punching the Heart
And kicking the Soul
Stop pointless banter
Get the ego in check
Focus on your gifts to give the world

Today is a new day
Today is a day to receive God's favor
Accept this with a Scream
A Scream of thanks and gratitude
A Scream of a new beginning
A Scream so LOUD
That ALL HEAR YOUR LIFE'S PURPOSE
AHHHHHH!

Piles of Ashes

Piles of ashes surround my memory
The future that once was
The love I thought I shared
The person I use to be
Are all a pile of ash
Burned to the tiniest remnants

Ashes give way to new growth
But only if there is true forgiveness
For if not a fire will ignite once again

Soul's Thumbprint

Our Soul is but a thumbprint
an identity.
By accepting who we are fully,
we place an imprint on our Soul.
Yet, many do not reach this acceptance,
carrying an illusion of who we are not
in our minds.
This is when the Soul speaks,
and sometimes screams,
it's language of pain.
Attempt to release your weary eyes,
from worldly bonds.
Realize your uniqueness,
and accept it Today.
Past condemnation locks
your Soul from moving forward
to place Its imprint on the world.

Tiny Mirrors

images of my life appear
on shattered glass
tiny mirrors in my mind
reflections of good times
and painful memories
they float like a cyclone
showing their reflection and then go by
only to follow the same course again

I try to form the shards
into a picture
of what my future holds
yet, the more I do
the faster they spin

You Might Feel Power

You might feel power
Through milestones and accomplishments
For what do they really tell?
Narrow slices of life
Power is like the sun, and
Even the moon
The sun is devoted to shine light
Everyday, even when clouds appear,
It still shines
The moon lights up darkness,
Whether whole or in part,
And shifts tides to kiss each shore
Past placards praising work
Yesterday or yester-year
Define worth, or contain power
Worth is humble efforts today
To shine light for all to see,
For all to grow,
To shift tides, irrespective of the storms
Brewing in the sky
Our challenge is not to be eclipsed
By our worth definitions
Rather, to shine power today
With integrity, grace, humility, and
To act on the sincerest love in our hearts
Towards every fellow man
Then, you might feel power

Heart Rungs

As I lift the cover to my heart
and climb down each rung,
I feel the turmoil built over time.
It speaks of uncertainty of who I am.
Archetypes have formed, molding
me, shaping my views.
They are hard to escape and
prevent me from knowing.
Who is the real father?
The guy playing catch or
the guy sacrificing for his clan?
Who is the real husband?
They guy who walks hand in hand or
the guy who suffers for his clan?
Who is the real son, friend, neighbor?
I am blind to these.
Who am I?

Take another step down the ladder
in my heart.
I can't see, but just feel.
Life is giving me the opportunity
to see, to believe.
But this damn archetype
shadows the clarity.
I know I am the son of God,
That love of me and others
is all that is asked.
But...!

Seek Who You Are

Seek who you are
in the glorious moments arising miraculously
and in the dredges of suffering.

Seek who you are
in your child's smile
and your partner's venom.

Seek who you are
in quiet times only hearing nothingness
and chaotic moments centered on nothingness.

Seek who you are
in the hand of your lover
and in the mirror of your darkness

Seek who you are
in each heartbeat, each holy instant, each opportunity
beautiful days offer.

Rightmindedness

Foolishness is wanting what is not ours
So we reach contentment
Foolishness is wanting the outside
To complete the inside
Foolishness is wanting our needs
To be filled by another
Foolishness is wanting what is lacking
Without being grateful for what is

Rightmindedness is receiving what is and knowing
God holds our intention to reach our full purpose
Rightmindedness is allowing our inheritance
To flow to us, and then freely giving what we received
Rightmindedness is wanting to give
To our brother in need of the God-self we possess
Rightmindedness is cupping salvation
In our hands and placing it in our hearts

There is No Need

You just need to be.
There is no need to be certain.
Certainty is being you.
There is no need to be a variety speaker.
Variety is being you.
There is no need to be significant.
Significance is being you.
There is no need to grow.
Growth is being you.
There is no need to contribute.
Contribution is being you.
There is no need for love.
Love is simply being you.

The tip of the root
From which the weed in the Soul grows
Is your own identity to the needs.

Holy Alter of Innocence

Deep within the kaleidoscope is a dot
The center, the core within all the images
As the hand twists, the images evolve
Never staying the same, just forming and dissolving
Within each one is also a core
A core of innocence, where
Happiness and contentment reside
Where "who you are" resides
As the hand of God twists life
Images form and dissolve
They dominate the view
Clouding the core, one is not the fading image
One's true identity is the core
That core is the holy alter of innocence

During the Walk

I am the fall color
I am the smile
I am the mountain
And the stream
I am the glory
I am the pruner
I am the father
And the voice
I am the blue sky
I am the rainy day
I am the cloud
And the victory
I am the garden
I am the bumble bee
I am the flower
Opening to light

Family Chain &
Archetype

Strong Like Wolves

Men, wake up
Our women are branching new flowers
Flowers of a new way,
New independence
Independence is taking new roots
In their souls
Souls guiding to more love –
A different love
Love they want from us, but love
They are not finding
Finding new fissures to seek the water
Their souls' need

Men, wake up
Climb from our roles and grow
Grow from the provider role,
The leader role,
Roles that are needed, but
Not like before
Before we hunted and gathered
Filling an archetype passed
By our fathers –
Be Strong Like Wolves
Fathers are now teaching the same
To their sons

Men, wake up
Be Strong Like Wolves
Be keen and swift
Work together for your pack
And don't carry yours alone

Gather and provide
See through all ranges,
But, gather strength from
Your women

Men, wake up
This strength is going to be different
We cannot rely on past roles
Passed down from our pack leaders
We need to provide what their
New independence needs
We need to provide an emotional connection,
A connection not watered down
By the stresses of the range

Men, Be Strong Like Wolves
But, be connected
Else your pack will head
A new direction,
Led by the independent woman

Family Chain

Divorce hit me with such
A force that it seemed
Natural.
Instinct kicked in as I
Hopped from grandparent to grandparent
Home to home, if they could
Be called such.
School was interesting
Catastrophic to say the least
Lost from who I was
What little I knew of me in a decade
Lost in fog
Where simple things like my age
Couldn't be remembered
Imagine that, such a quick and
Scarry change
That a kid forgets his age!
Oh, the laughter I endured
So much was lost
Homes and pets
Friends and teachers
Close connections and identities
Most of all lost opportunities
Opportunities that who knew
If followed
Where would life lead?
Am I better for it today?
One never knows
Now, my children are faced
With the same loss

Where could they have gone?
Are they better?
One never knows
Again, it seems second nature
The only option is to apply
Lessons learned
Hope the lineage breaks
Within the family chain

Boy to Man

The Boy, links of curls, freckles
A smile that beams
Trying his best to thrive, in confusion
Loss and pain of divorce
One step fighting forward
Ropes around his thighs
The weight is so much
Struggling at school, thinks he's dumb
Poor grades, remedial you are
There's no hug
Kids ridicule him, his name, his looks
Oogie-poopner, hahahaha, afro-boy
There's no hug
Fear at home, scared of him
Not sure how to love him
But does
Tries for a hug, go on now with a pat
Where's mom, she's gone, she's there
But gone
Her attention on the new him
Sad, no confidence, lonely, ridiculing
The rope is around the mind
Not sure how to love himself
But may
The smile, it still beams
It's all the boy has to give

The Man, widow-peaked, wrinkled
Ropes around the mind
Struggling to thrive, thinking he's smart
In confusion, loss and pain of divorce

One step fighting forward
Ropes of sabotage hold him
The weight is so much
Stay strong, be a good father
All he was, and he wasn't
Stay soft, be a good mother
All she could be, all she was
Don't be scared, as scared as he is
Sad, confident, lonely
But surrounded by loving
The smile still beams
As he gives

He closes his eyes
Recalls the boy, tangled hair
Freckles, playing alone
Hiding, but enjoying his mind's work
A tap on the shoulder
Come here, come to me
Holding himself tight, with a
Tight hold returned
Don't be scared, you are smart in so many ways
You are beautiful, loving
You are a wonderful son
Dad, I love you, don't be scared
Don't doubt your ways, your abilities
To love
Dad, you are what I need
Strong and soft, confident and nurturing
You are wonderful is so many ways
He goes back to play
There are smiles that beam

I Never Knew

There are fragments of your
life that I never knew.
Yet, I held you to be perfect.
I saw you make bad choices
that made me feel like you didn't care.
And, I held that against you.
I pushed you away
because I didn't want you to abandon me.
What good did it do to bury my hurt?
As you try to get close
I form a wall to keep you at bay.
Why do I resist healing?

I no longer see fragments
I see the truth.
Not once did I know you
were told you were not wanted.
That you were a horrible daughter.
How could you do better?
Now I want to pull you close
Help you forgive the lineage before.
Forgiving you will allow you to forgive her.
This wall has crumbled
and the bricks are strewn.

Who We Think We Are

As children, we incur wounds
Some laid intentionally
And others laid out of love
Each wound is a part of who
We think we are

Over time the wounds grow
They grow from our life reactions
To our child wounds
With each becomes a part of who
We think we are
Eventually the wounds need to heal
With the awareness of emotions
Running so deep
They strangle our heart

Adults, grieve your simple child wounds
As silly as it may sound
Be brave to release emotions formed
From scars of immaturity
With each release, we realize we are
Not who we think we are

The key to finding who we are
Is to see who we are not
What remains is you
Release your child wounds and all others
Will crumble to the ground

Truth Unfolds

Have you ever wondered how
truth unfolds?
Look on the past not with
resentment, anger, or guilt.
Not with hatred or confusion.
The past rolled you to this point
and it's all true.
What is not true are the illusions
created in your mind
about all the feelings blending
with the past.

Imperfect Soul

Close your eyes
Look into each chamber of the soul
The innocence of children's faces
The weathered faces of parents
Who did the best they could
The beauty in your lover's eyes
The memories of past teachers
The scarred walls of heart ache and loss
All make up the cosmic magic of your soul
All push and pull you to grow
Perfection of your soul
Lies in the imperfections
Of those working within

A Man's Heart

A man's heart, beats loyalty
and duty, for the little faces
that make up his dream.
Purpose is sometimes shadowed
behind the cloak of the day's
tasks and obligations.
Passion is often buried
under a heart of stone, hoping
time will one day present opportunity.
Vulnerability is quick to dissipate
when she needs to show her face,
as archetypes paint a different role.
Happiness is there to take
like a carrot on a stick,
with each day forcing a new step against.
Still a man's heart beats,
it's the awareness of the beats,
that bring to life all of these.

Our Play

Control, out of reason
Torrent beliefs create pockets
Of falsehood, illusions
Built from character
Trained by society, parents,
Influencers, and ego reactions
Our play unfolds
From what our eyes breathe in
And from thoughts manifested
Our play is not truth
Our play is a concoction
Of interpretation
An un-mortared, brick wall standing
On the foundation of youth

Scorns Our Men

Who scorns our men?
Versions of each other
Not versions of purpose
Who scorns our men?
Amplified expectations
From fathers and society
With well intent, but
Bindings that shackle purpose
Is the purpose only to provide?
Or is it the binding expectations
That scorns our men?

Judgement & Blame

Freedom from Chains

Freedom from chains
Self-imposed chains
From disconnection with source
Trying to control the uncontrollables
Is a chain
It's like paddling against a rushing river
To reach the adjacent shore
One can move through force
Using all his energy and
Closing his awareness
As he fights
One can chain his mind

I would rather float with the current
Bouncing over rapids
Staring at the clouds
Hearing birds sing the song of praise
As the current
Places me gently on the shore

Be Passer-by

Life comes at you like a river
Using force to gently press
Your constitution
Each ounce of fight shortens
The view of the river
For one's focus is on controlling

Be Passer-by
Allow the river to push you back
That may be the path upstream
Don't seek fancy vessels
To do the work for you, or
To disguise the work to be done,
As seen through another's eyes
Currents will increase
Sometimes near bends around which
You cannot see
It's all okay,
Because you are still in the river

Our Salvation

Internal salvation – the pent up
peace we all desire – is buried
under layers of non-forgiveness.

As we peel the layers away,
by forgiving All Others, but, most
importantly, forgiving Ourselves
for judging others, we come
closer to pure love.

This is how we can experience love
for someone we seemingly hate.

If we allow unforgiven layers
to wrap the hate,
like earth's rock wraps its core,
we can never reach the salvation
at the core of our soul.

Drifting

All events are separation
Separation from our connection with God
God says he will not forsake
Forsake us from our perceived ills
Ills that drive fear, guilt, shame, and other discomfort
Discomfort is our illusion
Illusions to show that what is perceived is not true
True, we feel these falsehoods
Falsehood around the emotions and separation
Separation never existed at all
All the time we had the opportunity
To live the peace of God
We just chose to drift from it

Cause Within the Mind

Our minds our powerful
They invent, and twist
They form illusions, and project
Imperfection
They dream of good, and
Worry from fear
Mostly, they create illness – pain!
Pain from feeling self-imprisoned
Lack, inferiority, angst,
Guilt, shame, and
Many other falsehoods
Pain is not a physical attribute
It's in the mind
Jusk ask, what is the purpose
Of this discomfort?
And you will be shown the
Cause within the mind

Climb Fences

Have you ever peered
through a knot hole
or a telescope?
There is a boundary around sight.
I once gazed at the moon,
focusing on craters,
not until I hit the perimeter
did a see a world of stars.
As I widened the lens,
my sight brought more wonder.

Avoid peering through knot holes
at distant objects,
future crossings,
or knot holes of loss, or pain,
or worry, or control.
What good is it to hike
if you stare at the trail?
Climb fences that block vision
so both eyes can see
all the looming possibilities.

Rose-Colored Glasses

For a moment today
look over the rims of your
rose-colored glasses
Surprised at the colors?
At what you see?
When did you put on these glasses?
Or, did they form their hue over time?
Truth is not the rose-color
Truth is the colors around the hue
The colors of peace

Release the Vice of Bitterness

Minds get trapped by unforgiveness
What is your vice of bitterness?
A childhood hurt, abandoned or chastised
A lost dream not meant to be
A partner who rejected your best
Perhaps your own condemnation swords
The repetitive vice of "if only" or "should have"
These lemons sour the mind
Lock out the world's joy
To loosen the vice, and dissolve it completely
Picture the innocent face in its most beautiful light
Bring forth the greatest image and smile
Feel the calmness in your heart as you say
"May you be blessed and loved"

Sword of Judgement

God does not seek retribution
There is no intent to punish
Correction from suffering
Involves suffering
If not, from where would the motivation
come?

Where resistance to suffering lives
So does resistance to truth
Truth is battled often within
The sword of judgement
The sword that deflects truth
Because there is a fear
To allow more suffering

The sword of judgement
Is only self-inflicting
Yet, it is easy to grab and swing
Its wounds are invisible
But have deep impressions on the heart

The master of the sword
Is a master of fear
Defensiveness is nothing more than
A shadow of one's imperfection
The shadow is behind the eyes
It's not seen until the eyes point inward

But why look inward
When the sword of judgement
Is so easy to swing?

Why accept imperfection

When the sword carves superiority?
We perceive

Why accept ourselves as clay
When there is not trust
In the potter's hand?

Why suffer more?

If we only understood
The suffering lives only when the arm grabs
The sword of judgement

As soon as we lay down the sword
The shadow comes forward
So we can accept the
Truth of imperfection
And God's gentle hand

Suffering & Solitude

Oh Seventeen ('17)

Oh Seventeen,
the unknown of you.
Carry me to new places
and follow what is true.

Winter solstice is here
with each day is more light.
Shine bright within me
as I gain more sight.

When new seeds sprout
As the ground loosens and bees rumble.
Let my heart warm
with grace that is humble.

When the sun is high
    and the days long,
soak each moment with gratitude
as it is the place where I belong.

Colors will change
as beauty takes new form.
Apply the lessons
as another year is reborn.

When days shorten
and white beautifies the land
feel blessed
that she is holding my hand.

Never Alone

Solitude on a lonely pond
Frozen waters of past
Support my feet
Cold winds shift my gaze
Thoughts of the coming spring
Of healing waters cooling my body
Cooling my mind
The ice enables me to walk
To the new shore
Realizing I am never alone

No End

Endings, whether it be suffering,
love, sickness, or life
are continuous.
Where is the end really?
Is the joy following suffering
a piece of suffering?
For without the anguish
joy would be unknown.
Is the remembrance of love,
the seemingly ended,
part of love?
Is the healthy life after sickness
really a part of the
healing process?
Is death the beginning
of life without?
Endings are imaginings.
They are bookends of time
placed by our minds.
Life and all its innerworkings
are timeless.
No end.

Solitude

Solitude, what I want
but when it's here, I drift lonely.
It's hard being alone,
after having companionship for life.
Sadness begins to wrap its roots
around my heart
ever so slowly, tightening around each chamber.
Solitude gives room for sadness to grow
and forces a face-to-face showdown.
This sadness is always there,
just more evident in silence.
The sadness speaks its purpose,
I just need to listen.
Today, it's because I doubt
others love for me.
False mind games resonating
from a childhood craving.
This is why I want solitude,
for the chance of healing.

Ripple

Each ripple of life is pushed by a wind
As ripples on a pond only exist with this energy
They cannot move alone
The ripples travel, and traverse new forms

Does a ripple suffer?
It has to
It is peeking from stillness
It is no longer tranquil
The wind dies, and it tries to
Settle back to calm waters
It knows tomorrow's wind will shift it again
It will raise up to suffer
So it can see from new angles

Maybe deep down it wants to
Be a wave, and crash into a new shore?
Even when this happens,
Suffering does not end

Blind Deaf Heart

With no eyes, nor ears, my heart
sits in solitude.
It speaks not from a tongue,
but from angst.
The language is not clear,
as my mind works the dream.
Yet, what it feels is right,
which is only uncovered through
my sight and my listening.
And, by translating its foreign tongue
into words that feed my soul.

A Star Shines

A star shines.
Angst from an unknown future,
And doubts of my abilities.
Locked in concrete
My feet won't take a step
Towards the shining star.
Efforts come and go
As I nudge forward,
With bursts of hope and faith,
Only to stop, and toil some more.
The star twinkles from afar,
Asking me to reach for it.
The concrete weighs me down.
"Focus on the lesson, not the hurt", I say
Awareness fractures the concrete
And the star brightens.
Surrender sheds the concrete
And the star drops within reach.

The Road to Truth

The soil crackles, stepping along
The Road to Truth
A road that is hard to follow
There is no path in sight
Each step lights only the new day
Leaving the wanderer time to soak in now
As soon as he tries to look ahead
Creating a map of illusion,
Or he tries to look back
Checking if he missed a turn
The light of day's step dims
To the point he can't see
The ground under his feet
We wish the Road to Truth was
Marked with golden light
And guides waving the way.

The Dark Friend

The dirt path presents my walk
This beautiful morning. Crisp air
Fills my lungs, and the warm sun
Shines over mountaintops
Warming my cheeks and lighting the way

The unknown – well not really –
Walks next to me
I see him on the ground, sometimes
Behind, and other times ahead. Irrespective,
He's with me – the one with no light

I ask him "What is it like
Living with no light?" He responds,
"But I do." The light is what makes me alive
We walk for a way, and then
The sun shifts to my back

Only the dark casting is in my gaze
He is leading the way. A different
Feeling when darkness leads
I wonder, do you have a heart?
He must. Then realize it's the heart of light

I wonder, if he had eyes
What would he tell me?
If he had a mouth
What would I hear?
But darkness only mimics to conceal light

So you are part of me
How do I know you? And
Should I hide? It's only

When you know me will you find
That there is no need to hide

I only speak through teachers
You know when I talk
The feeling arises, mistakenly thinking
It's the cause of the other
It's not their actions. It's me inside you

Morning Routine

The slowness of the morning
Is filled with sounds
Of songs from perches high in trees
Chirps, and pops, and melodies
Dance through the air
As the winged sit in their morning routine
It's as if the chance to sing
Is what gives peace, or
Confidence, for the day ahead
There is no desire to fly
Above the trees to see what's
Happening in the world
There's no rush to search for
Food, or fear to look out for prey
There is only the presence
To sing their song of joy

Calories Character Needs

The boy speaks, "My body is just my outer shell."
Facing death, he faces the loss of all
Does he?
Even when health diminishes and death is imminent
The terminal do not become sick in the mind
Or sick in the soul
Cancer touches no element of character
Divorce touches not one drop of character
Job loss, can't even reach character
Unless we allow them
Character is above these on the food chain of life
It feeds on sickness and loss
It grows to chase good, which is just
A few branches above
It eyes unconditional love at the apex
Will he reach it
Not without hardship
Hardship are the calories character needs

Magnet of Pain

Empathy is born
from understanding pain.
His shoulders are weighted
with the pain of others.
Like a magnet
desiring its opposite
his empathy attracts pain.
Without realizing, the pain
is swallowed to his belly.
The feeling, Aaahhh!
He just wants to scream out
as the pain digests.
Thoughts of weakness swirl
in his mind.
"He is weak because he didn't fight"
No, the pain landed, and
now he toils.
Unbeknownst to him
empathy sought the pain.
Empathy wouldn't know itself
without the pain.
Empathy wouldn't flourish
without nutrients from pain.
Empathy is born
mirrored to others,
maybe not to the pain projector
but to others.
He now understands
why he attracts pain.

Forgiving

The Boundary

A true boundary is an offer
of salvation.

To someone who has tested your
weaknesses and hurt you.

It's a kindness offer to your teacher
that releases them from
their pain.

The offer is the salvation, not
the outcome.

Because when you offer this, when you
offer love when you don't want to,

The salvation you receive provides
peace and thereby provides
protection to you.

The boundary.

Pebbles of Self-Esteem

Our self-esteem is a
Rock at birth
Slowly and unconsciously
The rock is chipped
Away by the patterns
Of our lineage,
As we are taught to
Protect and shelter
Eventually, the rock turns
To a pile of pebbles
With which we pave
Our roads, Roads of
Low self-esteem
Roads that carry us as
Partners and parents
To protect and shelter
Roads laid in waste
Of time misused
These roads must be lifted
With each pebble turning
Back to rock forming
Piles to love oneself

The Backpack

The backpack grew heavy
Its heaviness weighted
Each step on my journey
Each unforgiven encounter increased its
weight
I thought the weight made me stronger
But it held me back – slowed the journey
Unforgiven hurts of Mom and Dad,
Bullies and mean spirits
The unforgiven wound mate that was my
partner in life
Unforgiveness of myself – of my
Self-identified sins and failures
Stuffed the backpack to its brink
These seemingly deviations along my journey
Were checkpoints to my Father's
As I reach him, the backpack torn and tattered
I come in gratitude, holding a
Forgiven heart
The backpack now holds weightless images
Beautiful images, of Mom and Dad,
Them and Her, many of me
Each image is signed "The Best I could"
They stay with me in forgiven weightlessness

Glance of Guilt

"We are familiar with the guarded
glance of guilt"
The expressed face of shame
around floating eyes that avoid contact
Guilt is the acceptance of another's
projections, as no one can make us guilty
Guilt is a boulder from which
we cannot move to mountain tops
Guilt, like fear, angst, anger and regret
is a calling from the Soul
It's the Soul begging
to be in alignment
Behind every emotion is
a need for healing – embrace it!
Only then will we be able
to see from mountain tops

Contentment Breeze

As I release control of the future
As it glides on a breeze
To Heaven's gate
Contentment lifts my spirit
Losses were not losses
But gifts
Struggles were not struggles
But gifts
Fears were meaningless cogs
Shadows!
Restricting the heart and
Furrowing the brows
As I release
Cheeks take on the childhood softness
The world is vastly beautiful
Go into the dark to bring forth light
Allow the breeze to guide you
with contentment

Fear Binds Forgiveness Frees

Fear binds the world
Forgiveness sets it free
Why are we fearful to forgive?
Like a hardboiled egg, our fear
Has a hard shell
Yet, it's really thin, if one looks closely
Closely with faith that all will be okay
This outlook makes the shell
Easy to crack and peel away
Inside is a Journey to a yolky soul
The yolk of new life
Nature set protection around the soul
Knowing that one day
New life would break through
Our souls have the same fear coating
We just need to break through
By forgiving the past

Sorry Tear

A sorry tear is a special tear.
It streams cheeks only
When eyes can see straight
To a fracture on another's heart.
Sorry tears do not heal the crack.
They merely release
To show a lesson was inherently learned.

I Give You Permission

I give you permission
To have someone love you
To have someone cherish your beauty
And your spirit reaching for dreams
I give you permission
To bring in a partner
To support our kids in my absence
To honor their gifts
And cultivate their dreams
I give you permission
To be happy
To be in peace
And to love like you never have
Peace be with you, and live with ease

Two Hearts of Stone

Two hearts of stone
Come together in union
A purpose unrealized
Beating in their false images
And granite confines
They begin to fragment and crack
The stones' blood eases through
Trying to reform the wall
But the beats of time
Cannot endure the inevitable

Two hearts of stone
Shattered
Lying in the remnants
Now sand
Being carried away by waves
To the bottom of the sea
With each cleansing cycle
And each ray of light
Holding possibilities in its glimmer
Two hearts of flesh beat a new life

This Instant is the Only Time

Time contains past dealings
Time holds future worry
Blended to form illusions
To steal the Now instant
The speck of peace
That we can breathe in
The air of salvation saying
"all is well Now – forget it"
Not forgetting, or not forgiving,
Is a thief of the Now
And Now is the jewel of life

In the Shadow of the Moon

Our pain is great, but necessary.
You made my heart crumble,
and eyes weep deep sadness.
I did the same to you.
Our condemnation and resentment
ate the core of our connectedness.
Yet, we see love still sprouting
Like a Yew, discovering a new
plat for nourishment.

Our pain is great, but necessary
My heart longs for a deeper love for you.
It longs to dance a fiery tango with your soul.
Our commitment and passion
stir the core of our connectedness.
Seeing a new layer of love to reach for.
One we could have never touched.
Like a star flickering in a distant galaxy
hidden in the shadow of the moon.

Growing From Struggle

Cloud's Eyes

Tonight's dusk spawned
Violet and sapphire hues,
Cast over mountain ridges.
Captivated to the point
Of stillness, seeing peace
And tranquillity, or love
For the sun's departure
I wonder as I stare aimlessly
At the clouds.
Would they see the same
If their eyes cast upon me?

Unknown Road

Stand firm in shifting winds
against voices speaking
another's shortcomings.
Focus on horizons afar.
Breathe confidence, and let
the heart pound.
Exhale an almost silent growl.
Then take a step forward
on the unknown road
and dare not glance
in the rear view mirror.

Power Lies in Peace

Power lies in peace
Strength and confidence
Exude healing to others
Like a bear that grabs attention
From all of natures' eyes
He knows who rules his journey
And walks his path
Grounded strength
Healing others in his presence
Healing himself in solitude
Nurturing
Flipping rocks and foraging hives
Taking tiny speckles of nourishment
So his journey can continue

Life is Struggle

Life is struggle.
A seed fights through heavy soil
to taste light.
A butterfly battles through the chrysalis
to strengthen its wings,
so it can kiss flowers.
A mother releases pain from the
strength built during pregnancy,
so new eyes can cast on the world.

Life is struggle.
Without struggle there is
no room for growth.
There is no coming out of your shell
and no opportunity for re-birth of another.

Embrace struggle.
Knowing growth is taking place.
Each minute of effort
and ounce of pain
are proof you are living.

Hand on Our Back

We all need a hand on our back
The support and faith presses
Us forward, like a gentle breeze
Presses trees to shed their leaves
Sometimes it is necessary
To change our colors,
To wilt ever so slightly, and
Let go of the stem grounding us
In life, what is not growing is dying
There is no steady rhythm
Notice your colors are starting to change
Let them.
Then, let the hand – the breeze
Guide you

Truth is Shown

Everything we see
Everything we hear
Everything we read
Everything we speak
Is not true
All are illusions of one's mind
Expressed
Based on its perception

Truth is not known
Truth is shown
Ask for truth with awareness – listen
Then, and only then, will the
Holy Spirit go to work

Grady of Joy

Life is but a teacher
The classroom our eyes
Events are subjects
With each comes a lesson
Resulting in a grade of joy

Brick by Brick

Brick by brick I rebuild this
Shattered wall
Bricks of healing layer the floor
Bricks of forgiveness
Gratitude and contentment
Bricks of compassion
Peace and oneness

A new brick comes to hand
Like the others
It is chipped and dinged and scuffed
It has a new purpose
The mortar of life will fill in
These chips and dings
As they are necessary to
Create a tighter bond

As layer upon layer unfold
The wall's purpose resonates
Its job is not to keep out
But to contain

The Path

Just as the liquid of life
traverses its course through veins,
The Path to our father
is one in which each cell of consciousness
awakens to its light.

Though each journey varies
The Path's steps are the same.
Start now with acceptance.
Truth is!
Once you accept, you understand
your journey is from a lesser to a greater.
How fulfilling!

Wisdom now grows along The Path -
seeing past events as lessons
smartly placed for your benefit.
Wise souls know hatred, condemnation,
and other tenants of hell
are temptations to leave The Path.
Aim the sword at one-self.

The Path is atonement.
A revelation of perfect love.
The reflection from within,
to the outside and back.
Peace knowing all are sons of the father.
Innocent and born in love.

Father, grab my hand.
Let's walk The Path together.
Your will is now my will.

My will is our will.
Our will is The Path.

Many Possibilities

Each time we attach meaning to something
It's like we place that something in a box
With no room for further understanding
Because meaning is the end to possibilities
If were able to take that something out of the box
And look at it each day with fresh eyes
We would see many possibilities

The Purpose

Purpose does not scatter like the stars -
one for union, one for fatherhood,
one for career, one for material quests.
Purpose is not about me, or to get
what is lacking -
for if it were, purpose would end
once the time was met, or the object obtained.
This is how purpose and intention vary.
The purpose is to live your God-self
and shine that light as a partner,
or father, or colleague
all through life.
The purpose is to live in peace and gratitude –
on the highest peaks, in the darkest valleys,
along the steepest climbs, and during easy descents.
The purpose is to know God's hand
is on your back,
and that All Is Well.

Soul Tree

What about the leaf at the
top of the tree?
Is it the leader reaching towards
a new light, new possibility?
Or, is it the King?
No! Kings shroud themselves
in the center for protection.

Is the leaf different
than the deepest root?
The deepest root is grounded
in truth, in mother earth.

Or are they connected?
Does the root feed the ability
to reach new possibilities?
Maybe
Maybe its depth is what allows
the top to grow taller.

Where in the tree do the
nutrients from mother earth, and
the inspiration of light meet?
Where is the tree's Soul?

Where is yours?
Maybe it's all that exists between
the feeling of the ground
on your bare feet, and
the warmth of light
gracing your crown.

Maybe the entire tree is a Soul?

Accordance With Nature

Stormy winds pierce the mountaintop
Spruce bending, twirling
The only way to survive
Like the bear seeking shelter
Through the long winter
Or the flower opening her beauty
As the sun pours on her face
Man plots his course
A road created despite his knowledge
Smarter than nature – he thinks
He fights to not bend
Or go inward during seasons
That ask for nourishment of self
The light pours on his face
Yet, his beauty folds, as if hiding
Out of accord with nature
Absent from the God within

Gratitude

All is Well My Son

Always believe in the Beloved's will
Lighting love by forgiving core wounds
Loneliness is an illusion, a separation from God

Innocence is yours, as a child of the Beloved
Sins are here for you to forgive –
    you are imperfectly perfect

Wayward hearts, seek beats from within
External desire, shame, and fears
    set them afloat
Lessons are here for healing
Let them reign in your
    wayward ways

Many exclaim injustice as judgement of themselves
Yelling, kicking, and punching
    their own best efforts

Separation happens when control and
attachment take root

Oneness happens when faith, gratitude, and
    forgiveness shine daily
New days are coming, with new lessons and
    new miracles

Grace

Grace the presence of this Earth
as a ray of Sun,
for you are the son, yes, you,
the light who shines to all in need.
Each of us has grace.
It's whether we choose to live our ray,
to enable one to feel
the light of peace on our heart.

Beloved's Grace

I see the Beloved's Grace
not the hapless wanting of past lives.
I drink from a new spring
cooling my heart so my soul can fly.
My garden spawns flowers
allowing bees and hummingbirds to
share in my joy.
Sun, hit my eyes so I never leave
this Grace.
Blind my sight so vision is only ahead.
My garden is rich and is there
for all to love.

Gratitude Prayer

God, I greet the moment in the Holy Instant
Thank you for where my life is today
Thank you for all the beautiful people,
and opportunities in front of me
I have faith my future, and my
kids' futures, are in good hands
I will continue to forgive those
who harm me
And forgive myself for all my actions
that led me to where I am today
I am thankful for you closing doors,
and opening new ones
I will continue to prosper and
have abundance
I am one with you, and will live each day
as a reflection of you
Praise you God, this is my intention

Water on My Soul

Heavenly father
Rain on my heart
Let each drop fill my Soul
With your Will
Let me squeeze my Soul
And pour waters of love
On all who I touch

Flower

Your ray of peddles
A sight of beauty and strength
Feed so many
From the winged explorer
To the grateful eye
Your simple existence
Is one in which
We all should model
Standing each day
In our beauty
Patient and open
So each passerby
Can walk away thankful
From gracing our purpose

The Truth Is

I use to think my vocation
Was the key to happiness,
Fighting to have a dream -
Appearing in a crystal ball -
Become real, and then, I would be
In my Soul Purpose, I would be happy
The truth is, I want the peace of God
I want to follow his word
"Love when you don't want to love"
"Forgive when you don't want to forgive"
"Hold off judgement when you want to judge"
Here in lies the peace of God
Here lives my work, as any daily
Task is just a means
In this frame, miracles work a thousand-fold

Immense Gratitude

Immense gratitude,
Have you felt it?
No!
It lives in your heart,
sort of like an anxious feeling -
because of our perceived lack
keeping gratitude away.

It's funny, how immense gratitude
brings joy and peace.
Then suddenly another wonderful
connection, or a helpful nudge,
just appears, in its own
synchronous way.

What is Salvation, Father?

Salvation is living each day,
knowing all is well.
Facing problems and dilemmas
with poise and without attachment.
Breathing to release angst
and the emotions tightening your heart.
An unbending faith
that you will be provided for,
despite the circumstance
playing out in your mind.
Salvation comes when you connect
with me, and feel my hand
guiding you with firm resolve.

Blue Rabbit

Nourishing the mind
Nothing more than a box
Boxed in with devils inside
Looming to attack

The spontaneous rabbit
A great listener, turns blue
Steps close to the feet of the mind
Hoping the devils don't notice

The two devils certainly see
The bright blue rabbit
Trying to gain nourishment
A devil moves in, to attack

The foot gently compresses
The devil, pinning its intent
As the hand of God opens
The door, casting light and a way

The rabbit gladly exists,
Dropping the blue and
Meeting loyalty to the heart,
Steps at ease, away from the devils

Rest Softly on the Horizon
of a New Day

Intoxicated time fills the throat
With past drinks, clouding my head
Drunk thoughts meander
Around a cyclone of "what is right?"
"What is wrong?"
The real question –
What is now?

Nothingness.

Nothingness is sober, free to experience
The moon wheeling through a clear blue sky
Before it rests
On the horizon of a new day
Drink not regret or obligation,
Or even simple dreams of want, or lack

Drink only the breath of God's love –
Energy to the heart –
So it too can journey across a clear blue sky
And rest softly
    On the horizon of a new day

Love

The Poem of Amazing Love

This is the Poem of Amazing Love.
Love for the Journey, for the hurt,
and the days of confusion.

It's Love for the abandoner,
who does it in front of me, as she
abandons herself.

It's Love for the divorce
that stripped dreams, injected instability,
and opened the gates to –
This is how life is.

It's Love for the bullies and those
acting behind lenses of superiority
And for the man who believed in me
despite my blind self-bashing.

It's Love for the harsh father
with hidden gems of gentleness,
for his pain, and all those like him,
that he places on me without
a hint of awareness.

It's Love for the predator
trapped in his own cycle of hell,
using my body to explore.

It's the poem of Loving the greedy
who bring out my greed
in the light of our quests.

It's Love for the partner who
wanted what she wanted, but was unable

to commit to wanting me.

Meanwhile, it's Love for my unmet needs,
the things I wanted, but was unable
to find inside.

It's Love for the intentions behind the
marriage,
even though we didn't know the real
intention is
a relationship of purpose.

It's Love for all the striving to gain certainty
and the failures that said
certainty is not the way to
God.

It's Love for the days where I said
"Why is this happening?"
"What did I do?"
and for the days where my gifts
helped another find the
answers
to those very questions.

Oh yeah, it's Love for the teachers
who teach without knowing – the bosses,
and neighbors, the one who lives as if the
world
spins on his axis,
and the guy with no ripples
in his pond.

Speaking of teachers, this Poem would be
remiss
if it didn't mention the child

who teaches me my greatest weaknesses –
the gift that forces a deep
glance
in the mirror.

It's the Poem of Amazing Love
for who I am, where I am,
and the character shaping events
that guide, and continue to guide,
to what I Am.

A breath. An inhale of Love, and
a release of Love.
A breath Here and Now.
It's these Loves that allow me
to understand other Love.

The Love of the warm breeze on my skin.
The Love of a rolling stream,
where I sit still in silence.

It's the Love of all what nature provides
without waiting
for my permission.

It's the Poem about the Love I get
as I stare at the moon, the mountain
in the horizon, and the twisted
beauty within this flower.

And, it's the Love of holding my son
feeling his heartbeat, knowing
his heartbeat is of me.

This is the Poem of Amazing Love
that speaks through my pen and doesn't want

to stop writing about it.

Couples Dance

Couples Dance
through fields of joy
in taverns of worry
against steadfast walls
and in harmonious interludes

Couples Dance
to be one
to aim for one's dreams
tightly embracing one another
to reach a divine oneness

Couples Dance
in deep sorrows
around lost dreams –
at least they thought –
over rapids of pain
and in the face of endings

Couples Dance
in seas of tranquility
over mountains of hope
among fields of angels
and towards horizons of peace

Couples Dance
holding hopes firmly
and fates high
with committed hearts
while staring in each other's soul

Couples Dance their journey
because that's what couples do

Well of Love

My well of love is deep.
It swirls with a current
that's boundless.
As I courageously ladle
the love over you,
I see it sparkle in your eyes,
see it at the tips of your smile.
I see it wiggle in your toes,
and fill your soul.
I see it reflect back
as boundless as from
where it came.
I see my well become fuller
as it sits in your presence,
and as it remembers you when away.

Love Starved or Full

People say I'm love starved.
kids, family, clients,
and friends fill me
with love

Speaking "Thank You" causes
tears to stream.
obviously, I love me
and my blessings

I'm not love starved,
I'm love full.
just starved of the
right person to receive
my deepest love

The Soul Behind Them

Your eyes are beautiful
so is the face that holds them
and the soul that's
behind them

Follow Love

An impulse of love, if followed
wherever it leads, will become
richer and more intense, and
in the end will reveal itself
as divine

*Because I Already
Know I Love You*

You say let's not move in haste,
But, I already know I love you.
You say time can be at a slow pace,
But, I already know I love you.
You say you are excited and afraid,
But, I already know I love you.
You say you don't want to receive
a debt that has to be paid,
But, I already know I love you.

So, why should we wait?
Because I don't know I love me.
I say I have never really loved,
Because I don't know I love me.
I say I taught myself to feel inadequate,
Because I don't know I love me.
I say I don't know how to love a woman,
Because I don't know I love me.

Oh Dear God, teach me to love me,
Because I already know I love her.
Take the charge out of past losses,
Because I already know I love her.
Allow forgiveness, compassion
and gratitude to fill my minutes,
Because I already know I love her.

And, one more thing, Oh Dear God,
stand with me as I love her.

Float My Heart

The image of your laugh
floats to my heart
and fills it.

The image of your eyes
floats to my heart
and fills it.

The image of your hands
floats to my heart
and holds it.

The image of your nurture
floats to my heart
and holds it.

The image of our future
floats my heart.

Curl Your Everything

Curl your everything inside me
like a spiral
so a unit of conscious love
travels a limitless time
to a divine conscious love
only to end at the
pinpoint of my soul.

A Part of You

Let's not be apart!
Let's not erect walls
to separate or climb
Rather, let's erect walls
to contain.
Contain the specialness within
our souls,
The growth of beauty that is us.

I seek to be a part of you
as you seek me.
It brings tremendous joy to know
this part,
Great hope to embrace this part,
and solace knowing this part will flourish.

Let's not be apart!
Rather, let's be the sum love
of our parts.

I Welcome You Love

"Love waits on welcome, not time".
I welcome you love.
I welcome you to bridge
My heart to my soul
And my soul to my days.

I welcome you love to my oneness,
My spirit in a holy instant.
I welcome you love to flow to her
With sincere honor of her
Gifts and beauty.
I welcome you love to travel back
And fill my well
So it can pour out again tomorrow.

When We Love

When we make love
It's like I'm holding an Angel
In the Palm of my hand
Our eyes meet and my heart is full
Our bodies glide together
In soft waves
The sounds are songs of release
Of joy making sensations
Heighten to bliss
Never have I felt love so pure

Picture of Us

Your words soothe me
Like the presence of your
Heart pressed against mine.

Your smile pierces me
Like a ray of sun
Flowing energy to my soul.

Your coming excites me
like the greatest
Anticipation of childhood Christmas.

Your hand in mine bonds me
Like a grip not willing to let go
Of a never-ending journey.

Your love for me completes me
Like a missing puzzle piece
That is needed so all can see
The beautiful picture of us.

Happy Is an Inside Job

Today's messages are around what's missing
Find a new job.
Make a bucket list.
Move to a new place.
Change your home.
Find a new partner.
Wrong!

These are all grasps to an external.
It's trying to paint the car a new color,
While the engine remains busted.
One can't transplant an unhappy heart,
To a new body, and be Happy!

The pursuit of Happy has formed
A new Industry
The media scorches messages,
Messages that are attractors
To motivate change.
Messages they create as if the creator
Is some mystic warrant of attention.
Remember, Happy is an inside job.
This is why we see those with nothing
Happy.

The rules for this job are simple.

Love the Oneness – with your God –
With gratitude and contentment.
Love Yourself –
with compassion and non-judgement –
You are a gift to accept.

Love All Others – for who they are –
Forgive their view of the world, and
Accept their level of consciousness – ego.

Allow All Others To Love You –
It's a mirror reflection
Of your love and a
Testament you are greater
Than Happy.

You Are Love.

Love for You

Being in love is when I can sit alone
far away
and bring up your face with a smile
causing and excited tension in my heart
and feeling grateful for knowing
all will be well when we meet again

Before I Die

Before I Die,
I want to smell a sweet scent
And smile with you.

Before I Die,
I want to love the textures of the
Beautiful painting of our unknown future.

Before I Die,
I want to hear us sing a divine praise
Of the love we share.

Before I Die,
I want to live a life with you that is
Richer than the cream in our souls.

When I Die,
I want to die with you
Pulsating one final synchronous heartbeat
With mine.

Live Soul Love

Life!
A grain
of sand
spinning down
a riverbed
lodging under
granite rocks
then shifting
free to
float with
currents

Soul!
The undercurrent
guiding the
grain through
each journey
shaping it
as it
touches others'
Souls forming
its own
alchemy

Love!
Living soulful
for another
for yourself
testing will
and growing
with grace

facing imperfection
with the
hand of
divinity

Love is a Free Gift

Love is a free gift
a silent whisper and gentle
touch from the heart
without worth or accomplishment
or sweat or sacrifice
love is there for all to open
never requiring any type of
production

Miracles

Miracles are like a bird's song
as they float through the
clear morning sky
to the light of the sun.

My heart today is a miracle.

It sings a song so beautiful
it lights the world around me
and all those who
wish to share the miracle.

Angel's Wings Patter

Two birds dancing in the blue sky
Against budding mountain sides
Over New England meadows
Gliding with warm light
On their backs
Seeing what lies ahead
And beneath
Knowing angel's wings
Patter with them

Scarlet Nights

Scarlet nights bring wonder
is it spirits returning
from a good day's work?
Is the image of the setting sun
supposed to draw in now?
Is it a glimpse of Heaven's
presence?
To me, the scarlet is a reminder
that light shines beauty
on every cloud

Sparkles

Sparkles glitter over waters moving out to sea.
They live at the tips of stars,
And within snowflakes beautifying the land.
Millions of sparkles enliven the world.
Their purpose, to highlight and bring to life,
As they shine on a wonderer's eye.
No sparkle compares to the sparkle in your
eye,
When your gaze sees the love in our hearts.
Your sparkle lifts me to new possibilities,
New sense of wonderment, and new fields of
joy.
It tells me your heart is pure, and ready
For my love.

Our Dance

Climb onto my toes
I'll carry the weight of your world
in my strength
Grab a hold of my waist
and pull me close
Put your gaze into my eyes
Let your smile crinkle
So I can see the light of happiness
in your soul

About The Author

When I was ten-years old, my parents divorced. It was quick, shocking, and took my life on a tumultuous path. It created difficult challenges, seeded my personal shadows, and shaped my scarcity thinking. As much harm as it caused, it also created great benefits. Resilience became part of my character, and I would need this as I faced my own divorce transition.

I, unconsciously, entered adulthood on a mission to prove my self-worth. This came in the form of career accomplishments, validation from clients, financial account balances, and a stiving to be a model father, partner and provider. Perfection was the driver. Underneath it all lied a barrier to me seeing my true soul's purpose.

The ending of my 20-year marriage gutted me. It was the final straw, in a string of ignored life lessons, that put me face-to-face with my lying self. My divorce created the inevitable showdown with my soul, and God, that I had been running from my entire life.

Tired of living with fear, angst, anger, jealousy, bitterness and unforgiven containers of hurt, I decided to begin a journey to find and establish a deeper spiritual connection.

My spiritual journey is great and quite eye-opening, but is far from over. Luckily, it's taking its own sweet time and presents me even more lessons as I unwind the complex grip my ego has on me. The self-reflection and space I created to connect with my spirit resulted in these poems. They are what helps me understand the false perceptions that guide my life. I hope they speak to you too.

Personal Life

I'm writing this from my home in Vermont. I'll be married, to my beautiful life partner and "Goddess" Samantha, within a month of writing this sentence. My three boys are now teens, and I try as best I can not to disrupt their soul's journey with my □.

Oh yeah! Then there are the three dogs, Greta, and the brothers seen above, Oscar and Rye. Border Collies are the best. The pups love to hike, bike, and *play soccer*, which is the phrase they associate with any ball being launched for an ensuing chase.

Mission To Change Divorce

The legal process around divorce is man-made and lawyer refined. Its hyper-focus on resolving family and financial matters solely is an incomplete view of what divorce is and what it entails. Yet, many associate divorce as these two pieces.

Quite frankly, the legal process is a breeding ground for contentious relationships to become more contentious. More evident, the legal process inserts a long window of distraction, leaving the divorcee reeling in other elements of divorce well after the process is over. This is the *"traditional path"* through divorce

The true nature of divorce happens both internally and externally. Internally, it scars the heart and creates conflicts one's soul must resolve. The answers will never come from winning a legal battle, or by securing the coveted marital wealth. The answers only come through self-reflection and intentional work to understand the complex emotions that arise.

My next book will center on helping divorcee's understand the harmful faults within the *"traditional path"*, and encourages them to take an *"unfamiliar approach"* so they can not only achieve the best possible outcome, but also, grasp the miracle lying within.

It's a book that steps beyond the material and takes them into divine guidance. It shows them how to approach divorce properly, and how to invite this difficult transition to uncover hidden pathways towards personal growth.

My Other Work

In addition to writing, I provide coaching services for those who want to move through and beyond divorce in a healthy way. You can find out more about the coaching services through www.youtreecoaching.com, or by listening to my podcast *"A Man's Journey Through Divorce"*, which you can find on Apple, Google, iHeart, and Spotify.

You can also connect with me through the *Spirit Poems Facebook Page*, https://www.facebook.com/sschleup. I would love to hear how the poems made a difference in your life.

One More Thing Before You Go…

If the poems touched you, and helped ease a struggle you're facing, then they can help someone else. Help that person find the poems by writing a short review on Amazon.

Thanks again for your support!
Steve